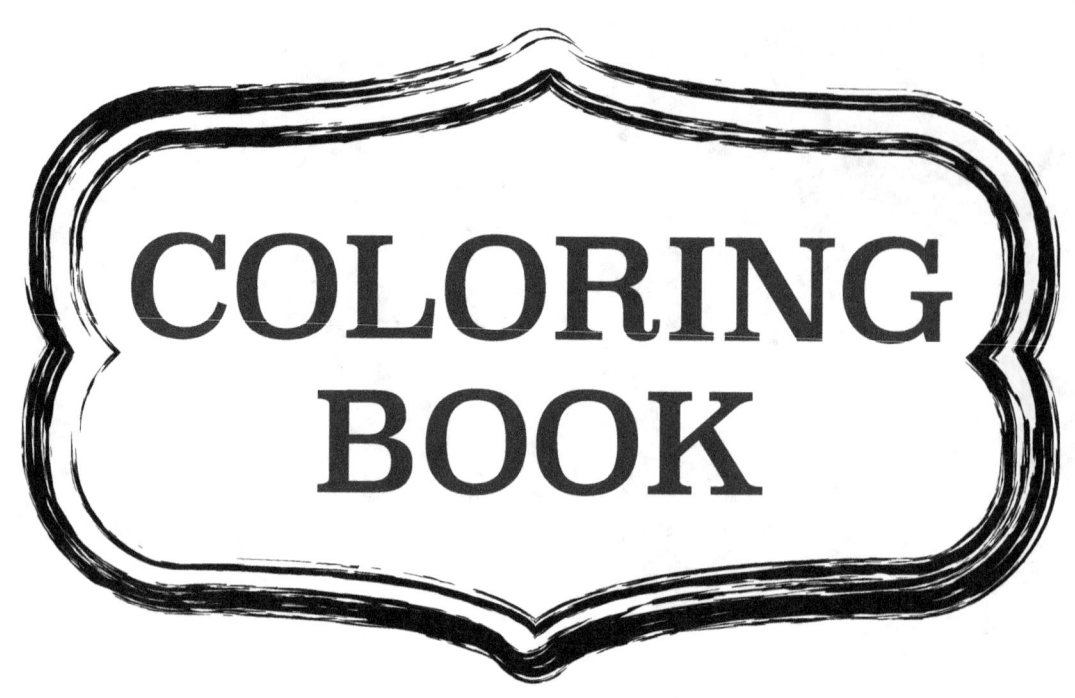

This book belongs to :

_____

_____

_____

_____

ZAZLUXE

Copyright protected. All rights reserved
Electronic or printed reproduction is prohibited
without written consent from the author

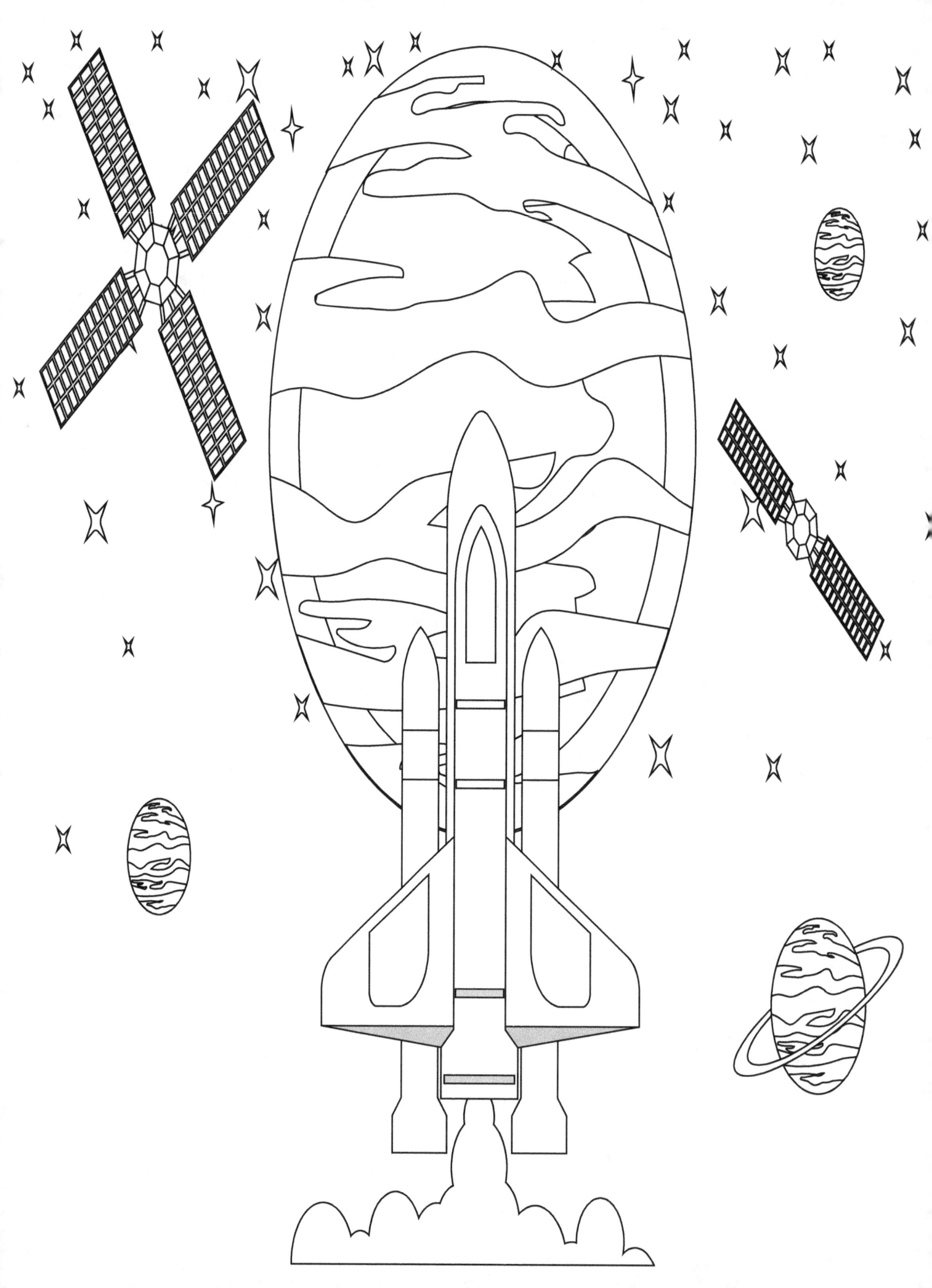

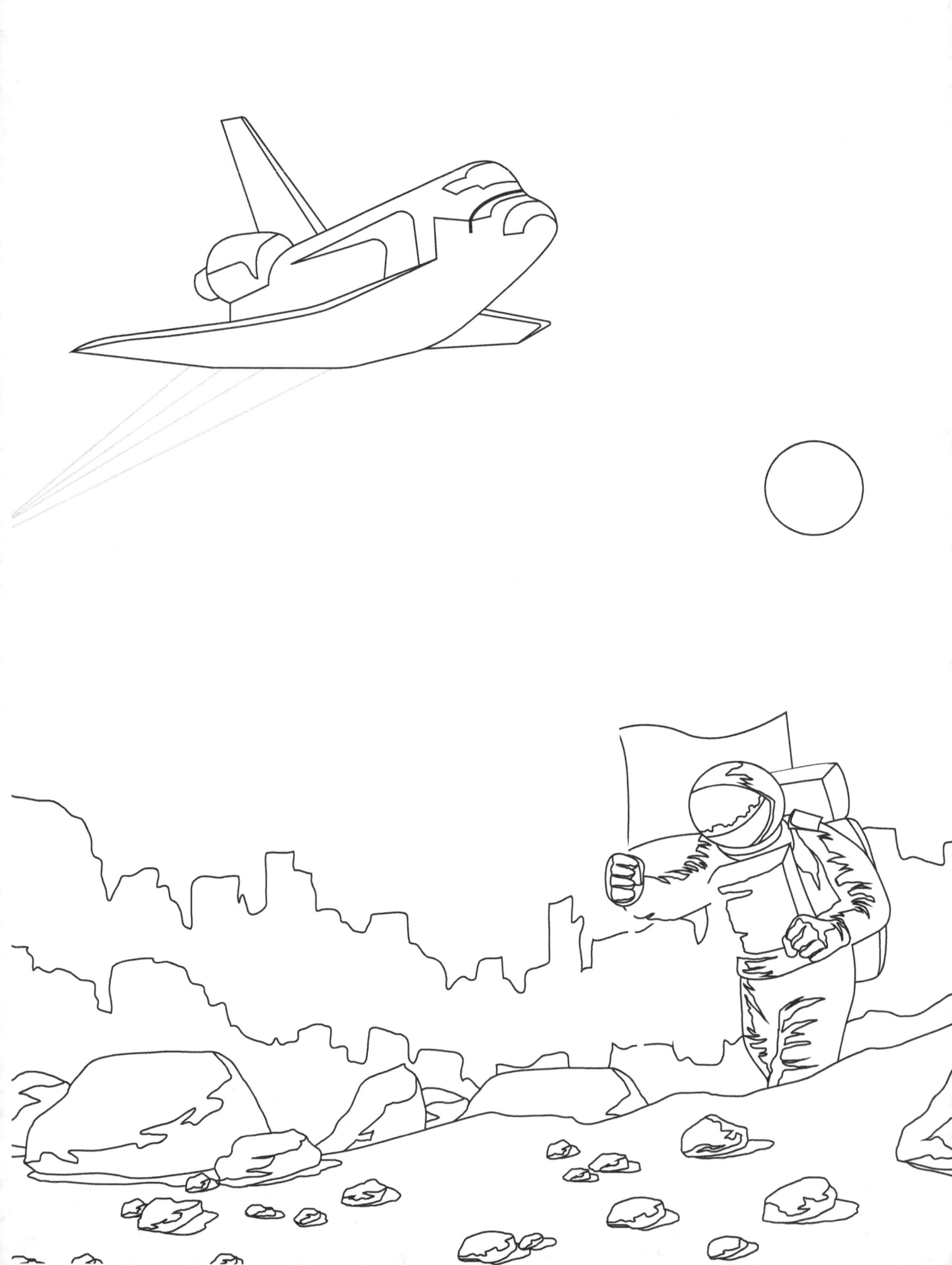

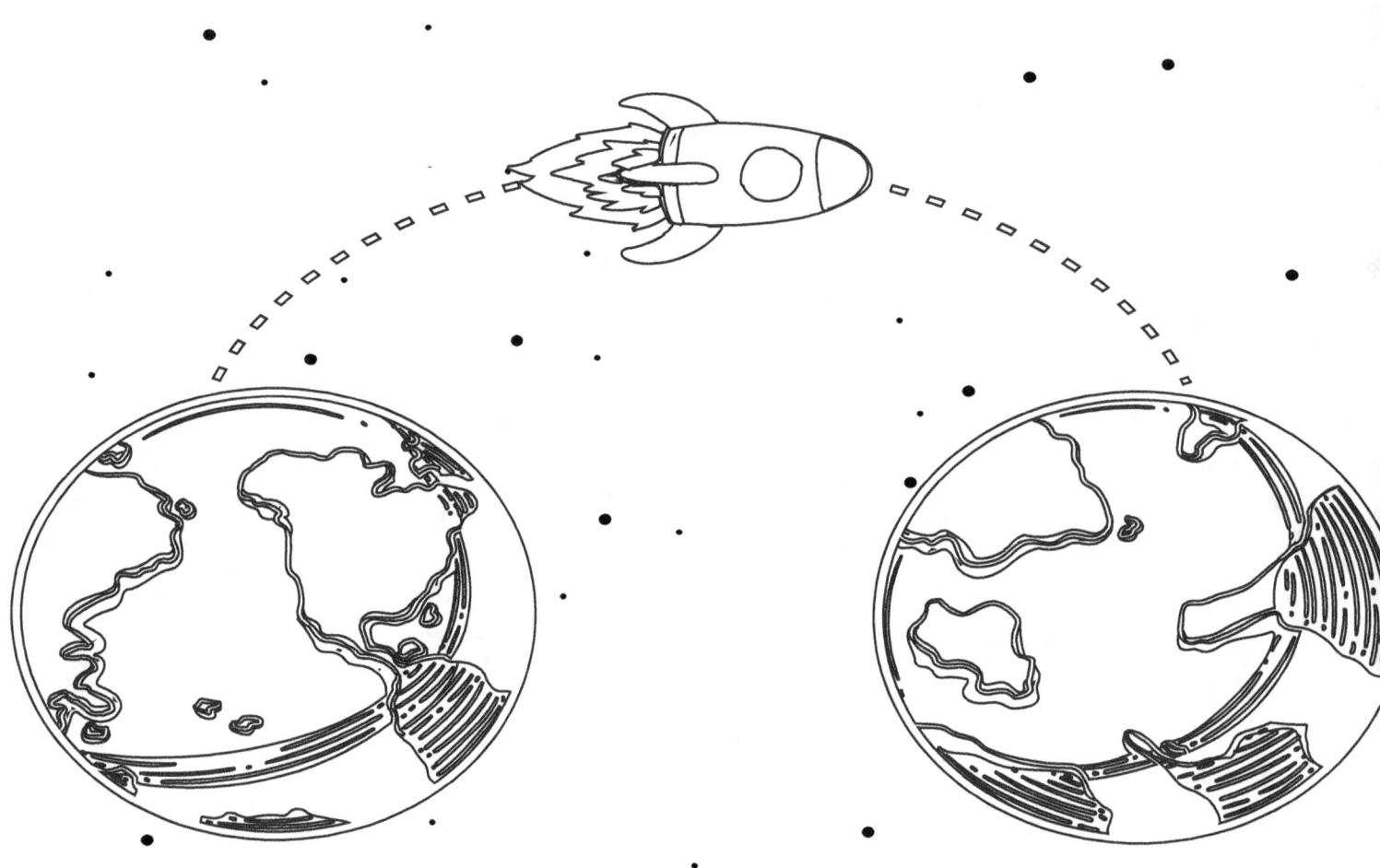

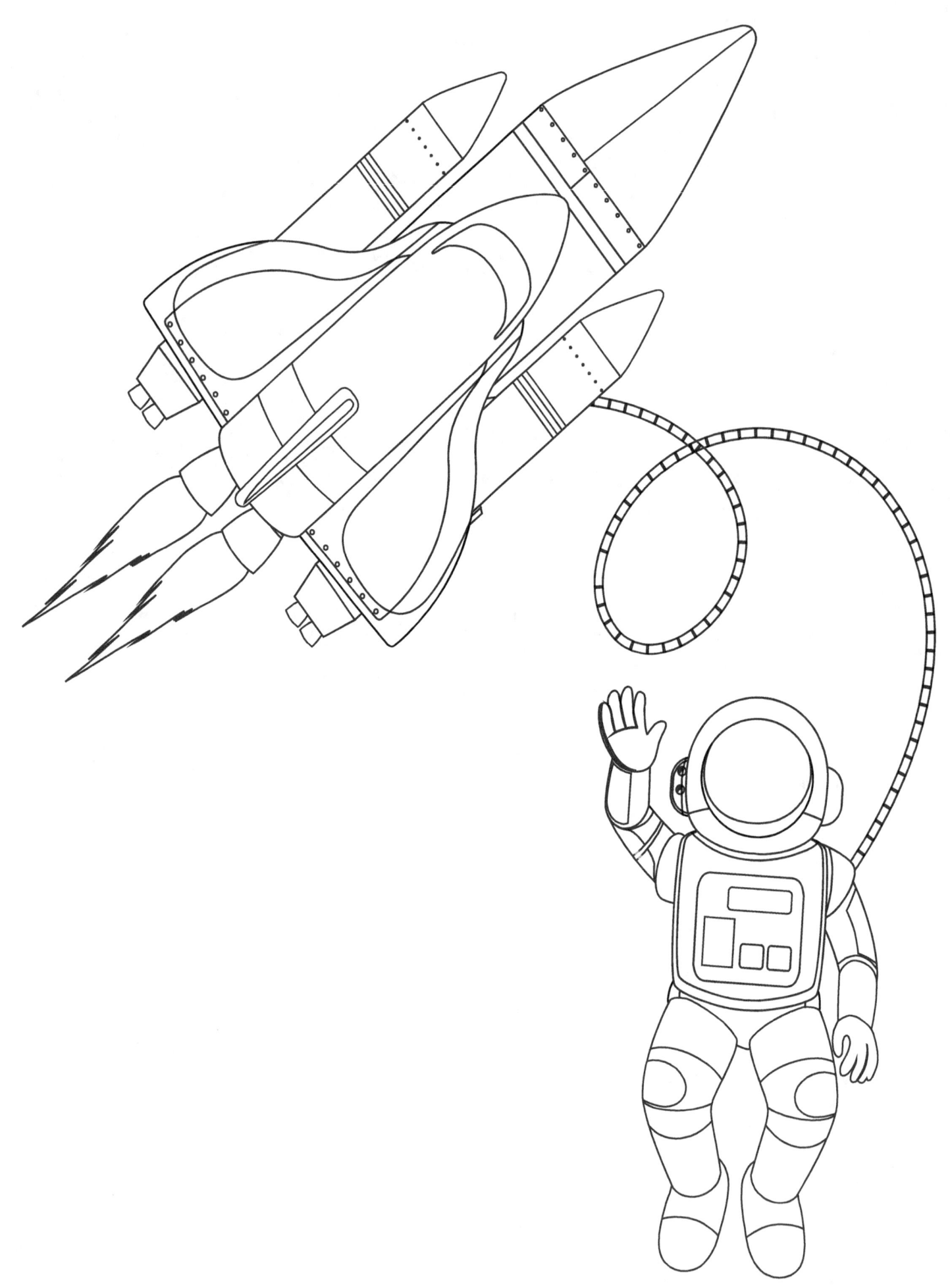

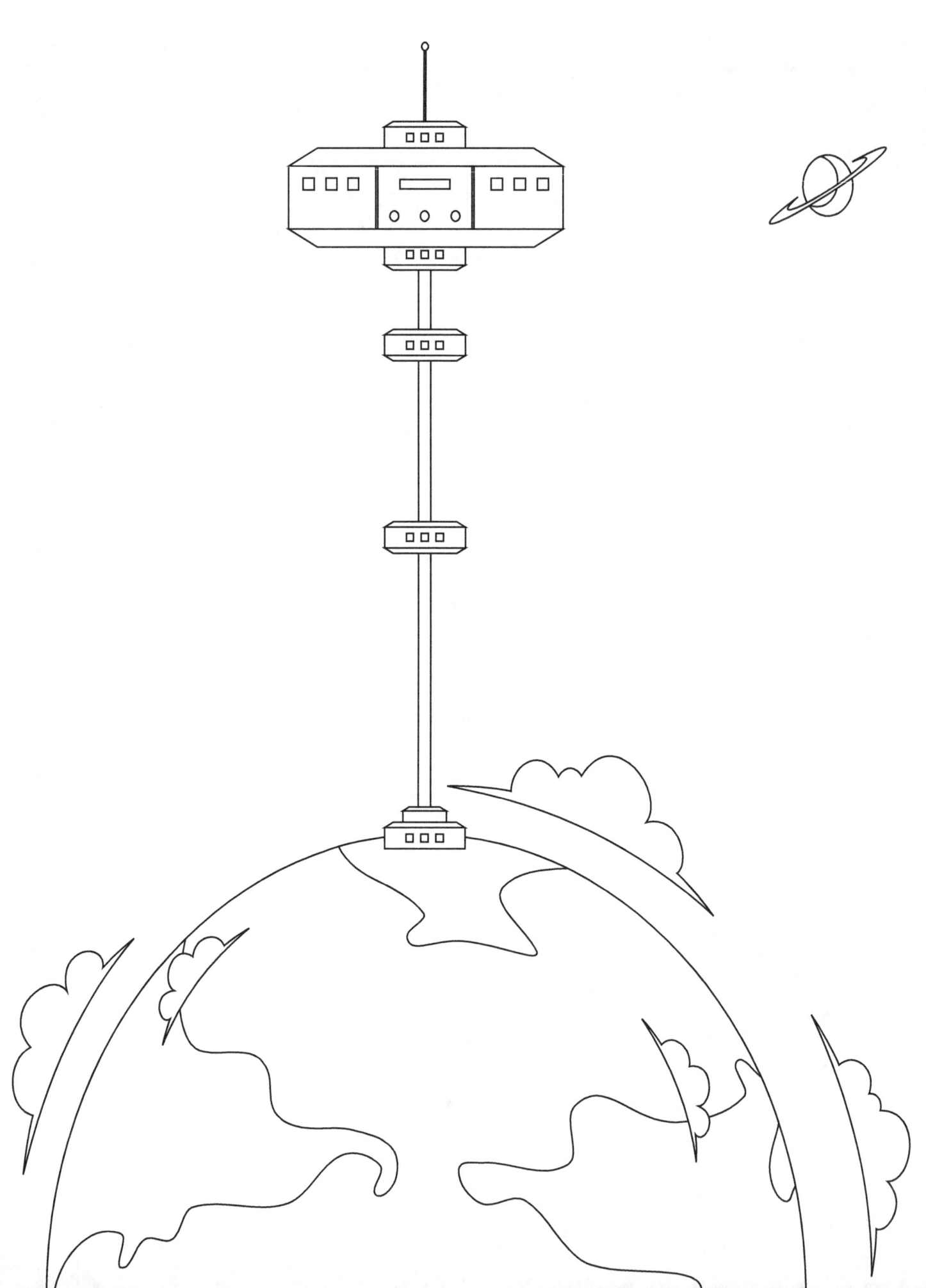

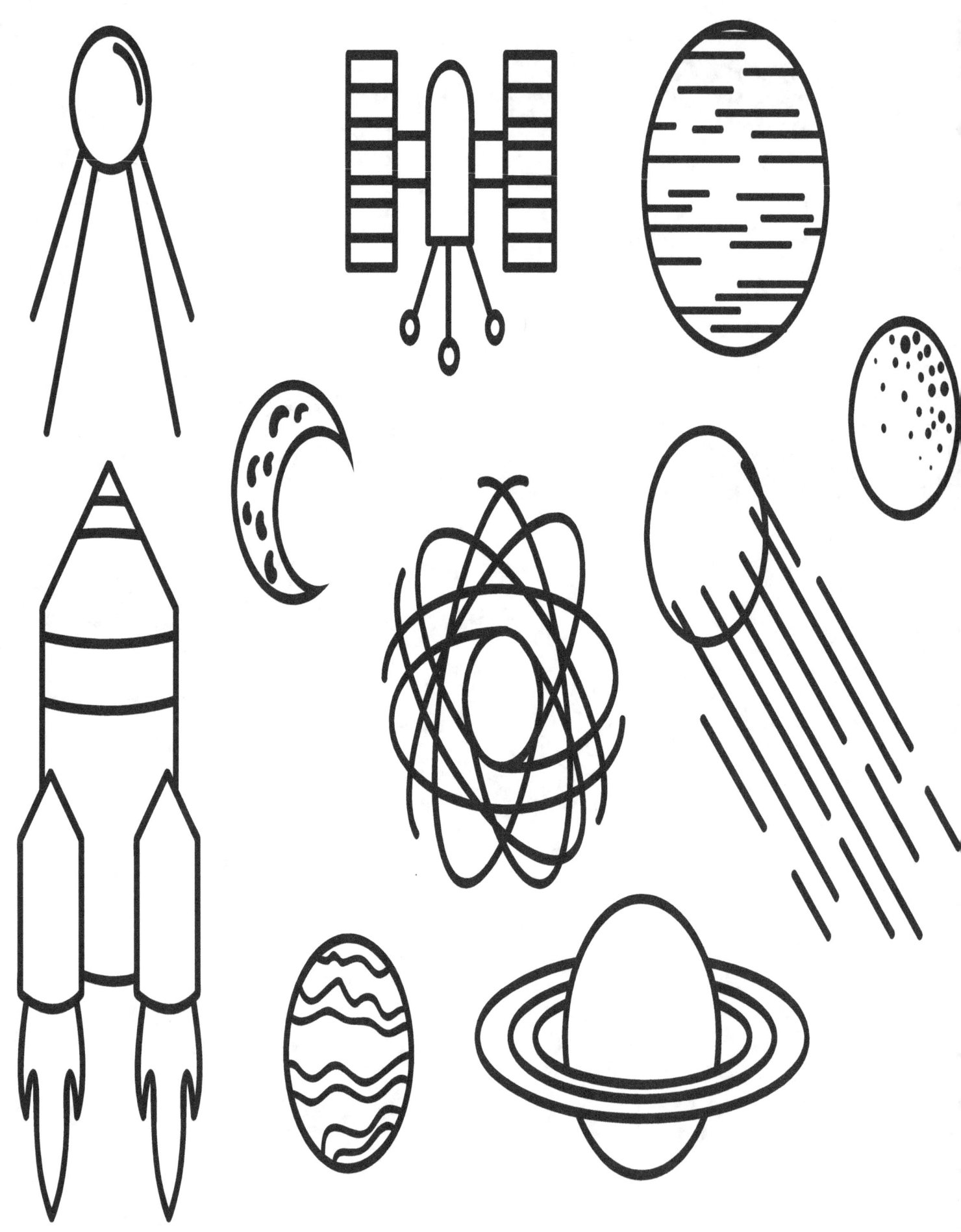

ZAZLUXE

Copyright protected. All rights reserved
Electronic or printed reproduction is prohibited
without written consent from the author

www.ingramcontent.com/pod-product-compliance
Lightning Source LLC
Chambersburg PA
CBHW081656220526
45466CB00009B/2780